Stranger Gins

50
things to drink
while you watch TV

compiled by
Carol Hilker

DOG 'n' BONE

Published in 2021 by Dog 'n' Bone Books
An imprint of Ryland Peters & Small Ltd
20–21 Jockey's Fields   341 E 116th St
London WC1R 4BW   New York, NY 10029

www.rylandpeters.com

10 9 8 7 6 5 4 3 2 1

A CIP catalog record for this book is available from the
Library of Congress and the British Library.

ISBN: 978 1 912983 41 4

Printed in China

Senior designer: Emily Breen
Art director: Sally Powell
Head of production: Patricia Harrington
Publishing manager: Penny Craig
Publisher: Cindy Richards

NOTES:

Recipes make enough to serve 1 unless stated in the individual ingredients list.

Measurements are occasionally given in barspoons, which are equivalent to 5 ml or
1 teaspoon.

Ice cubes or crushed ice are not stated in ingredients but are useful for most recipes.

All fruit and vegetables should be washed thoroughly before consumption. Unwaxed citrus
fruits should be used whenever possible.

All eggs are large (US) or medium (UK), unless specified as US extra-large, in which case
UK large should be used. Uncooked or partially cooked eggs should not be served to the very
old, frail, young children, pregnant women, or those with compromised immune systems.

Both American (Imperial plus US cups) and British (Metric) measurements are included in
these recipes for your convenience; however, it is important to work with one set of
measurements and not alternate between the two within a recipe.

CONTENTS

INTRODUCTION

In the pre-pandemic days, cocktails were a big part of socializing. Many of us were spoiled by the ability to have a drink after work with co-workers, share gossip over a bottle of wine with our best friends, or toast to exciting things with family for a celebration; but then everything shifted. And seemingly overnight. We all went from making weekend plans to hoarding toilet paper and Clorox wipes.

With sheltering in place, many were forced to get creative with their social lives. We Zoomed and House Partied and played Bingo and did online group karaoke, but as spring moved on, most of us turned to binge-watching. Maybe it was listlessness. Maybe it was what we were all familiar with, and it felt like the only normal and comfortable thing in a year of abnormality.

Once we started bingeing, we watched everything we could get our hands on, from throwbacks from the 1980s and '90s to re-watching some of the best shows of the last year (if not the last decade), to—let us not forget—murderous tiger keepers. For many of us, TV became our escape. Maybe even, dare I say, our fun.

This book is the perfect pairing for those homebodies out there, who now consider an episode of *Game of Thrones* or a rerun of *Cheers* to be their favorite sort of Happy Hour.

simple sugar syrup

Before we start, here's a recipe for simple sugar syrup, which is a key ingredient in some of the cocktails that follow.

Mix superfine (caster) sugar and water in equal quantities by weight and stir. The mixture will be cloudy at first but keep stirring and eventually it will form a clear syrup. This will keep in a clean, screw-top jar or bottle in the fridge for three weeks.

Ingredients

Superfine (caster) sugar

Water

carrie's cosmopolitan

Glass

Martini

Garnish

Orange peel

Ingredients

2oz/60ml citrus vodka

¾oz/25ml orange liqueur

¾oz/25ml fresh lime juice

1oz/30ml cranberry juice

This drink and this show go together like Mr. Big and Carrie, Miranda and Steve, and New York and money. When *Sex in the City* first aired, no one expected it to be as huge as it became. It also seemed that there were a few supporting characters that gained fame off the show. No, I'm not talking about Stanford or Aidan or Muffy, I'm talking about Manolo Blahnik shoes and Cosmopolitan cocktails. Carrie's Cosmo is now iconic among the most classic of cocktails made famous by pop culture.

Pour the vodka, orange liqueur, lime juice, and cranberry juice into a cocktail shaker filled with cubed ice. Give the contents a good shake to chill everything down and fine strain into a pre-chilled Martini glass. To finish, squeeze the peel over the glass, rub it around the rim, and then place it in the drink.

screwdriver

Glass

Highball

Ingredients

1½oz/35ml vodka

1 cup/250ml of orange juice

Ice

For the ladies serving time in Litchfield Penitentiary, there really is no piece of contraband more useful than a screwdriver. Whether they are using one for business or pleasure, the inmates in *Orange is the New Black* show real ingenuity. This now considered classic cocktail's origins can be traced a few decades back to when U.S. workers in the Persian Gulf would sneak vodka into their orange juice on the job... having no straw or spoon handy, they would stir the drink with a screwdriver.

Fill the glass to the top with ice. Pour the orange juice into the glass of ice. Pour the vodka into the glass. Stir (not necessarily with a screwdriver.)

SHAMELESS

dublin drop

The Dublin Drop is less Frank Gallagher and more Lip, Fiona and Kevin, and Veronica. (It'd be a little pricey for old Frank.) The drink combines Guinness (stout beer) and Irish whiskey to make for a curdling combination fit for only the hardiest of stomachs. In the early to mid-2000s, these Droppers were all the rage in Chicago bars, making them a likely pick for the younger generation of Gallaghers & Co.

Pour equal parts Bailey's and Irish Whiskey into a shot glass. Half-fill a pint glass with Guinness. When ready and moving quickly, drop the shot glass into the Guinness and drink the shot as quickly as possible.

Glass

Pint and shot

Ingredients

Makes: 1 Drop (because drinking alone seems very Gallagher-like)

½oz/15ml Bailey's Irish Cream Liqueur

½oz/15ml Irish Whiskey

A can of Guinness

slow run on the beach

Glass

Highball

Ingredients

Makes: 2 glasses

2oz/50ml coconut rum

1oz/25ml peach schnapps

1½oz/40ml
pineapple juice

2oz/50ml orange juice

3½oz/90ml
cranberry juice

½ teaspoon vanilla extract
(optional)

Baywatch **definitely had a lot of sex on the beach. No denying that! Buxom ladies and buff dudes saving lives with lots of slow-mo jogging on the sands of Santa Monica, California was the premise of the show that "ran" eleven seasons. Pair that with exciting storylines and it's the perfect quarantine staycation. To binge** *Baywatch***, there is no more refreshing mixed drink than the Slow Run on the Beach, something no show has ever done better than** *Baywatch* **did.**

Fill two highball glasses to the top with ice.
Fill a large cocktail shaker with ice and add the rum, schnapps, juices, and vanilla extract (if using).
Put the lid on tight and shake vigorously.
Pour evenly over ice in both glasses.

CHEERS

screaming viking

In season six of *Cheers*, Carla challenges a new bartender named Wayne, that someone will come into the bar that evening and order a drink he doesn't know how to make. To which he replies, "Impossible", so she bets Sam's boat versus Wayne's job that he will be stumped on a drink. In walks Norm and he orders a "Screaming Viking". Wayne insists it doesn't exist, but loses the bet—and his job.

Glass	Ingredients
Highball	2oz/50ml Pimm's No 1
	1 cup/250ml lemonade/ lemon soda
Garnish	
Apple slices	3oz/75ml ginger beer
	cucumber slice
	lemon slice
	orange slice
	fresh strawberry
	fresh mint sprig

Build all the ingredients in a highball glass filled with ice. Stir gently, garnish with apple slices, and serve with two straws.

dirty don martini

Glass

Martini

Garnish

Lemon-zested rim

Green olive

Ingredients

3oz/90ml gin

½oz/15ml vermouth

2 teaspoons olive brine

If you want to throw them back like a 1950s advertising man in downtown Manhattan, there is only one drink that comes to mind: the Dirty Don Martini. Like Don Draper (and other Dirty Dons who hail from New York), it's less pure and a lot more complex than it first appears. Served shaken, not stirred, and often consumed as and for lunch, (along with a cigar) there is no more versatile drink. Just make sure you add three olives, as Frank Sinatra said, "One for me, two for my lady."

Add the gin, dry vermouth, and olive brine to a cocktail shaker filled with cracked ice. Shake sharply and strain into a chilled Martini glass that you have wiped around the rim with a lemon zest. Garnish with a green olive.

danish bloody murder

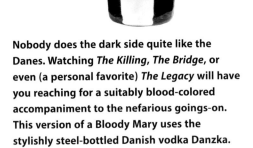

Glass

Highball

Garnish

Celery stick

Lemon wedge

Ingredients

1oz/30ml Danzka
Danish vodka

4oz/120ml tomato juice

2 pinches of black pepper

2 dashes of
Worcestershire sauce

2 dashes of Tabasco

2 dashes of lemon juice

1 barspoon of
horseradish sauce

Nobody does the dark side quite like the Danes. Watching *The Killing*, *The Bridge*, or even (a personal favorite) *The Legacy* will have you reaching for a suitably blood-colored accompaniment to the nefarious goings-on. This version of a Bloody Mary uses the stylishly steel-bottled Danish vodka Danzka.

Add all the ingredients to a shaker filled with ice. Shake gently and strain into a highball glass topped with ice. Garnish with a stick of celery and a wedge of lemon.

red wedding blood martini

Glass

Coupe

Garnish

Orange peel

Ingredients

3oz/75ml vodka

1oz/25ml Campari

½oz/15ml
raspberry liqueur

1 teaspoon fresh
lime juice

2oz/50ml cranberry juice

Winter is coming, so you'd better get some Vitamin C in first. This blood-red Martini should also put you in the mood for another viewing of the goriest nuptials in television history.

Add all the ingredients to a cocktail shaker filled with ice. Shake sharply and strain into a frosted coupe glass. Garnish with a strip of orange zest, twisting it to release the oils—it really does make a difference to the flavor.

THE CROWN

gin & it

Glass

Rocks

Ingredients

3½oz/90ml gin

1oz/25ml Dubonnet

Lemon wedge

2 large cubes of ice

This cocktail is perfect for a *The Crown* watch-party. While there are many drinks fit for royalty, the most royal of all is the Gin & It, a favorite of Her Majesty the Queen. The cocktail is seven parts gin to two parts Dubonnet and it's served along with ice and lemon. Dubonnet is a Parisian aperitif that is sweet and fortified with herbs, wine, and spices. To get the full experience, throw on your fanciest and sparkliest tiara and tune into *Downton Abbey*, just as the Queen does herself.

Fill a shaker with ice. Pour the gin and Dubonnet into the shaker and stir until everything is nice and chilled. Fill a rocks glass with two large ice cubes and a lemon wedge. Strain the cocktail into the rocks glass, over the ice and lemon and serve.

harvey wallbanger

Sure, there are tons of shows based around home improvement, remodeling, flipping houses—you name it. But *This Old House* is the O.G. of all things tool-time related. Since its humble beginning in 1979, it's been helping people learn how to build and maintain their homes. For many, being sheltered in place has inspired lots of DIY projects including painting, organizing, and for some, pulling the trigger on some long-needed renovations. The most appropriate cocktail for binge-improvement of *This Old House* is the Harvey Wallbanger (also a treasure brought to us from the 1970s).

Build the ingredients over ice into a highball glass, stir, and serve with an orange slice.

Glass

Highball

Garnish

Orange slice

Ingredients

2oz/50ml vodka

½ oz/15ml Galliano

orange juice, to top up

the copy room

Glass

Martini

Ingredients

3oz/75ml dry martini

2oz/50ml vodka

freshly squeezed juice of ½ lemon

3 teaspoons caster/ granulated sugar

3 barspoons balsamic vinegar

6 strawberries, puréed

This is the type of cocktail you can make again and again, even if it leaves you with a bit of a hapless morning the next day. You make it so much that your friends think it's obscene. But you're like, "Leave me alone, I just want to have a drink and watch *Suits*." Using vodka, balsamic, strawberry, and a splash of lemon, this cocktail is both adventurous and tart. It is the perfect accompaniment for watching *Suits* holed up in your house, alone, hiding from your friends... and annoying co-workers.

Combine all the ingredients and serve over ice in a martini glass.

Pictured opposite, left.

mon chéri

Glass

Martini

Ingredients

2oz/50ml Grand Marnier

1oz/25ml rum

2 tablespoons finely grated bittersweet/dark chocolate

½ oz/15ml cherry liqueur

2 barspoons cider vinegar

If you are going to binge on *Drag Race*, you should include a sleepover. This sleepover should have plenty of opportunities for pampering, and also a tray of freshly mixed Mon Chéris in honor of Rochelle Mon Chéri. Rochelle was the second queen to enter the competition in season two and left her mark on *Drag Race*. Her namesake mixes rum, Grand Marnier, bittersweet chocolate, cherry juice, and apple cider vinegar and is as decadent as the queens who "werk" the stage.

Shake all the ingredients together and serve with ice.

Pictured opposite, right.

sweep the leg

Glass

Rocks

Ingredients

2oz/50ml Sauza
Hornitos tequila

1oz/25ml Midori

1oz/25ml fresh lime juice

Many drinks could be enjoyed with the hit-action series, *Cobra Kai:* Coors Light beer, a Mai Tai (it rhymes), whiskey, red wine... but this show, with its diamond-in-the-rough lead Sensi, deserves its own drink. The Sweep the Leg is so named because it will put you on your butt if you have too many of them, but it's also a fitting homage to the Cobra Kais: flashy and a little sweet, but they will sucker punch you and the next thing you know, you'll be waking up with a bad hangover and at least a little lingering regret.

Add all the ingredients to a shaker filled with ice. Shake sharply and strain into a rocks glass filled with ice.

justice for barb

What else really needs to be said. *Stranger Things* **fans everywhere were left demanding "Justice for Barb!" aka the beloved Barbara Holland, whose life was taken so young and tragically in that pool! Thankfully, season 2 brought that resolve to fruition. This drink is perfect for a** *Stranger Things* **binge. The float of crème de mure provides the perfect special effect for enjoying the upside-down.**

Build the gin, lemon juice and sugar syrup over crushed ice in a rocks glass and stir. Drizzle the crème de mure over the ice and garnish with a lemon wedge and a fresh blackberry.

Glass

Rocks

Garnish

A lemon wedge and a blackberry

Ingredients

2oz/50ml gin

1oz/25ml fresh lemon juice

2 barspoons sugar syrup (see page 7)

½ oz/15ml crème de mure

 **OUTLANDER**

the fraser

Glass

Rocks

Ingredients

1¼oz/30 ml Scotch whisky

1¼oz/30 ml Drambuie

orange zest, to garnish

Using Scotch whisky, Drambuie, and a little bit of orange, the Fraser is definitely one for cold nights and blazing fires. This body-warming concoction is named after the *Outlander* leading fella, Jamie Fraser, the man that married WWII nurse Claire Randall finds multidimensional love with in her time travels to Scotland in 1743. *Outlander* is a television show made for watching over a long weekend, snuggled under a blanket.

Add both ingredients to a glass filled with ice and muddle with a barspoon. Garnish with orange zest.

beam me up, scottie

Okay, so maybe it's just a take on the classic cocktail the Aviation, but Beam Me Up, Scottie is cleverly re-named after one of the most popular TV catchphrases of all time. The show and the cocktail are both tried and true classics. Seeing as there are so many versions of this vintage drink, it's the most fitting of concoctions to sip, no matter which generation of *Star Trek* you decide to explore.

Put all the ingredients in a cocktail shaker along with some cubed ice. Give the ingredients a hard shake for around 15–20 seconds, until the contents are chilled and the ice diluted to take the edge off the alcohol. Fine strain carefully into a chilled cocktail glass to remove any particles of ice and lemon. Garnish with a twist of lemon zest.

Glass
Martini

Garnish
Lemon twist

Ingredients
1½oz/35ml gin

½oz/15ml lemon juice

½oz/15ml maraschino liqueur

Dash of crème de violette

chardee macdennis

Glass

Coupe

Ingredients

2oz/50ml gin

⅔ oz/20ml fresh lemon juice

2 barspoons raspberry syrup

a dash of organic egg white

sugar syrup, to taste (see page 7)

The Chardee MacDennis is just the kind of drink one would expect to order in Paddy's Pub. It's strong, loud, and might leave you acting a little obnoxious, which makes it a likely staple for Paddy's drink menu. The brightly-colored drink would also be the perfect accompaniment to an at-home version of "Game of Games."

Add all the ingredients to a shaker filled with ice and shake sharply. Strain into a chilled cocktail or coupe glass.

To make a Royal Clover Club, use an organic egg yolk instead of the egg white. This changes the color to a rich, orangey pink.

the mary berry

When the world seems unhinged, many people retreat to things that provide comfort, and for some that is baking. It seems like this year many found solace from the confinement of their kitchens. While there are many cooking-show TV heroes, no one is as universally loved as the UK's Mary Berry. This refreshing drink, true to its name, is a muddle of fresh berries, lime, and vodka. It is the perfect flavor pairing to a baking session in the kitchen, while bingeing just about any and every season of *The Great British Bake Off* or *The Great British Baking Show* in the background.

Muddle all the ingredients in a rocks glass with a wooden pestle. Top up with crushed ice and stir gently to mix. Serve garnished with a few fresh berries skewered on a toothpick.

Glass

Rocks

Garnish

Fresh berries

Ingredients

2oz/50ml vodka

4 lime wedges

2 white sugar cubes

3 fresh berries
(strawberries, raspberries,
or blueberries)

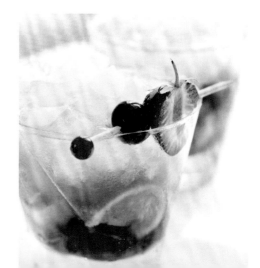

something blue

Glass

Margarita glass
or punch cup

Ingredients

2oz/50ml
reposado tequila

²⁄₃ oz/20ml blue curaçao

²⁄₃ oz/20ml triple sec

freshly squeezed juice of
½ lime

Every wedding must have the following: something old, something new, something borrowed, and something blue—preferably involving tequila. This is the perfect drink of choice for any hen or bachelorette party. The cocktail is two parts tequila with a bit of blue curaçao, and triple sec, shaken with ice and served along with a few bad decisions.

Add all the ingredients to a shaker filled with crushed ice. Shake and then strain into a frosted margarita glass or punch cup.

carole fu$%*ng baskin

What would we have done during lockdown without the distraction of Joe Exotic and the cast of characters in the Netflix TV show, *Tiger King*? For about a week, this show really took the world by storm and showed a real interesting side of Florida. Joe Exotic made this cocktail's name famous during the first few weeks of lockdown. It was the phrase he used countless times to explain how he felt about his arch-nemesis, Carole Baskin, a woman he would eventually try to have murdered. For your next *Tiger King* binge, have a Carole Fu$%*ng Baskin and have a nice day.

Layer each ingredient on top of each other over a barspoon in a shot glass.

Glass

Shot

Ingredients

½ oz/15ml Kahlúa

½ oz/15ml Baileys

½ oz/15ml Grand Marnier

the baby blue

Glass

Rocks or tumbler

Garnish

Grated nutmeg

Ingredients

1 sugar cube

2oz/50ml boiling water

2oz/50ml whiskey

This drink isn't really blue, but it does involve a little bit of science and a few small metal tankards. Named after the final scene that played with the Badfinger song "Baby Blue" in the background, this drink is a fitting way to re-watch one of the most popular TV shows of the early 21-st century. Plus, Jesse would definitely not consider it a "b*tch drink."

Warm two small metal tankards. In one, dissolve the sugar in the boiling water. Pour the whiskey into the other. Set the whiskey alight and, as it burns, pour the liquid into the first tumbler and back, from one to another, creating a continuous stream of fire. Once the flame has died down, pour the mixture into a warmed glass, and garnish with a sprinkling of grated nutmeg.

sour derby

This aperitif uses a well-balanced amount of bitters and aromatics to create a perfect drink to end a long day. The Sour Derby is an update on a classic cocktail from the 1930s, the Horse's Neck, which also seems like a fitting name for a crime drama featuring a gang of illegal bookies in post-WW1 England. "You can change what you do, but you can't change what you want." Sometimes all you want is a stiff night-derby.

Glass	Ingredients
Highball	2oz/50ml VSOP Cognac
	10 drops of
Garnish	Angostura bitters
Long lemon or orange zest twist	ginger ale, to top up

Prepare a tall glass with the garnish of a long twist of lemon zest. Fill with ice cubes and add the ingredients; then stir. Replacing the traditional lemon garnish with a twist of orange zest will add a subtle difference in flavor to this old-timer.

tequila sunrise

Glass

Highball

Garnish

Orange wedge

Cocktail cherry

Ingredients

1oz/30ml tequila

½oz/15ml grenadine

3oz/75ml orange juice

The heart and soul of the Oppenheim Group is their ability to sell amazing properties in Hollywood to the rich and famous—homes that most of us could never dream of owning. This sunny drink is an ideal way to enjoy the cut-throat drama of the Hollywood real estate firm. Similar to the cut-throat cast members of Selling Sunset, this drink is one part crazy, two parts classic, and served unmixed.

Fill a highball glass with ice cubes and pour in the tequila and the orange juice. Next, slowly pour in the grenadine, which should just sink to the bottom of the glass, giving the sunrise effect. Garnish with a wedge of orange and a bright-red cocktail cherry on a stick.

seis compadres

Many friendships have been solidified over a night of tequila drinking. For many, the sneaky liquor has provided a great accompaniment to the memories one may make with friends and roommates. Some good memories, or—if the tequila was cheap—some bad memories. In any event, when it comes to the six besties in the cult-classic show *Friends*, this drink is absolutely applicable. Technically speaking this drink is a Tres Compadres, but it uses six ingredients, making it a Seis Compadres.

Add all the ingredients to a shaker filled with ice. Shake sharply and strain into a chilled margarita glass edged with salt. Garnish with a lime wedge.

Glass
Margarita coupe

Garnish
lime wedge

salt, for the glass

Ingredients
2oz/50ml gold tequila

⅔ oz/20ml Cointreau

⅔ oz/20ml Chambord

1oz/25ml fresh lime juice

⅔ oz/20ml orange juice

⅔ oz/20ml
grapefruit juice

the wagon wheel

Glass

Highball

Ingredients

2 lemon wedges

2 barspoons caster/
granulated sugar

2oz/50ml Jack Daniel's

lemonade, to top up

If you aren't watching the hit FX TV show *Justified*, **you are missing out. The long-running American western crime drama tells the story of Deputy U.S. Marshal Raylan Givens. This hometown cocktail would likely be a favorite of the characters in Harlan County. The Wagon Wheel mixes Jack Daniel's and lemonade, for a refreshing way to warm up or cool down, whichever you might need.**

Muddle the lemon and sugar together in a highball glass. Add ice and the remaining ingredients. Stir gently and serve with two straws (optional).

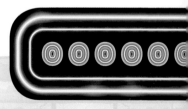

death in the afternoon

This classic cocktail was invented by Ernest Hemingway and aptly named after his novel of the same title. It's the perfect midday escape from the dark moments that life throws at you, and its ingredients (good absinthe and even better champagne) match Jen and Judy's friendship: strong, bubbly, and possibly dangerous (especially with good absinthe.)

Glass

Champagne flute

Ingredients

1½oz (35ml) absinthe

5oz (125ml) very cold champagne, to top

Pour the absinthe into a chilled champagne flute and top gently with the champagne. It will turn milky and opalescent. Serve immediately.

rambling rose

One of the best episodes of *Schitt's Creek* is "Wine & Roses", in which Moira Rose makes a commercial for Herb Ertlinger Winery, a local winery specializing in fruit wines. We won't ruin the rest of the episode, but this "fruit wine" cocktail was made in homage to one of the funniest moments of *Schitt's Creek* history, drunk or sober. There's no better drink than this to have in your hand, while watching this episode or the whole season.

Add all the ingredients to a pitcher/jug filled with ice and stir gently to mix. Serve in ice-filled glasses, garnished with seasonal fruit.

Glass
Highball

Garnish
Seasonal fresh fruit

Ingredients
(serves 4–6)

1 bottle crisp dry white wine

⅓ cup/100 ml elderflower liqueur

⅓ cup/100 ml dry vermouth

⅓ cup/100 ml Cointreau

3oz/75ml fresh lemon juice (about 2 lemons)

generous 1oz/30ml sugar syrup (see page 7)

2 heavy dashes of grapefruit bitters

the bad place

Glass

Highball

Garnish

Redcurrants

Ingredients

2oz/50ml gold tequila

½ oz/15ml fresh lime juice

½ oz/15ml crème de cassis

ginger ale, to top up

If someone ends up in the bad place, let's hope it has a bar. A play on a Dark and Stormy, The Bad Place is served up in a highball glass. It's a fitting drink to pour after an extra-bad day, when you need a tall one. Plus, one thing can't be denied, it's a forking amazing libation.

Build all the ingredients in a highball glass filled with crushed ice. Garnish with a small bunch of redcurrants and a devil fork swizzle stick.

manhattan

Glass

Martini

Garnish

Orange zest

Ingredients

2oz/50ml rye whiskey

½ oz/15ml
sweet vermouth

½ oz/15ml dry vermouth

a dash of
Angostura bitters

For a big ole' Mrs. Maisel inspired bash, bake up a pan of macaroni and cheese, mix up some nuts, and put together a few Manhattans.

Add the ingredients to a mixing glass filled with ice (first ensure all the ingredients are very cold) and stir the mixture until chilled. Strain into a frosted martini glass, add the garnish and serve.

BABY SHARK

the earplug

Glass

Shot

Ingredients

Whatever you can find in a crisis

Each generation has its annoying children's music. This one is no different. The drink pairing for *Baby Shark* via YouTube Channel is really anything you have on hand, any drink of your choice, anything you can reach while WFH. The key is to take a quick drink between each chorus of "Baby shark, doo, doo, doo, doo, doo, doo." While the song never quite loses its monotony, you may find the shots help inspire soothing dance moves between videos.

sea breeze

This Bravo reality show has been making waves since 2013. With lots of steamy drama set against a backdrop of the Caribbean, the Bahamas, the Mediterranean, Saint Martin, and Tahiti, it's hard to pick just one cocktail to sum this show up. The most nautical selection would be the Sea Breeze. At first glance, this cocktail is really just cranberry juice, grapefruit juice, and vodka, but shake it up with ice and you'll get a foamy surface on this summertime favorite.

Pour the vodka into a highball glass filled with ice. Three-quarters fill the glass with cranberry juice and top with fresh grapefruit juice. Garnish with a lime wedge and serve with two straws (optional).

Glass

Highball

Garnish

Lime wedge

Ingredients

2oz/50ml vodka

⅔ cup/150ml cranberry juice

2oz/50ml grapefruit juice

lime wedge, to garnish

FLEABAG

hot priest

Glass

Highball

Garnish

Lemon slice

Ingredients

2oz/50ml sloe gin

⅔oz/20 ml fresh
lemon juice

a dash of sugar syrup
(see page 7)

soda water, to top up

With a cigarette in one hand, a cocktail in the other, and no regrets, the heroine in *Fleabag* is a reminder to all that sometimes it's okay to be a bit of a scumbag, as long as your heart is kind of in the right place. This drink, the Hot Priest, is tasteless in description, but quite the opposite in reality. In the TV show cans of gin and tonic are the "tea" of choice for Fleabag and her Hot Priest. This gin cocktail, while not in a can, offers a bit of fizz and carbonation to the mix.

Add all the ingredients, except the soda, to a shaker filled with ice. Shake sharply and strain into a highball glass filled with ice. Top with soda water, and garnish with a lemon slice.

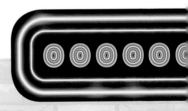

the villanelle

Glass

Rocks

Garnish

Stemmed cherry

Ingredients

2oz/50ml vodka

1oz/25ml Kahlúa

¾oz/25ml light/
single cream

The Black Russian is a dead-on name for this drink fit for an assassin. It's simple, classic, and will keep you on your toes, just as if you were trying to escape a dangerous killer! Whether you are a *Killing Eve* fan or not, The Villanelle is the perfect nightcap for anyone who likes their coffee black. This drink pairs best with an all-night binge-fest, when you don't have anywhere to go for a few days.

Shake the vodka and Kahlúa together over ice. Strain into a rocks glass filled with ice. Garnish with a stemmed cherry.

PIctured opposite, left.

AMERICAN HORROR STORY

election year

While one could argue that an ice-cold Corona would also suit a binge-fest of Ryan Murphy's hit ensemble show, *American Horror Story*, the appropriate cocktail for *AHS: Election Year* is undoubtedly a White Russian. For a US election season twist, add one teaspoon to taste of pumpkin pie spice. The vodka, coffee, and cream are the perfect combination of stimulants to stay awake through all the scary parts, whether it be on Netflix, Hulu, or real life.

Shake the vodka and Kahlúa together over ice. Strain into a rocks glass filled with ice, then layer the cream into the glass over the back of a barspoon. Garnish with a stemmed cherry.

Pictured below, right.

Glass

Rocks

Garnish

Stemmed cherry

Ingredients

2oz/50ml vodka

1oz/25ml Kahlúa

¾oz/25ml light/
single cream

all in the family

Sugar and mint mixed together with Bourbon are all you need to make this sweet Southern drink. While one might picture the Byrdes being more the mint drink people, this cocktail is dedicated to the Langmore family. It's sweet and a bit muddled—just like Ruth. The All in the Family is best suited for a summer day, sunbathing and plotting your next big crime… or maybe just enjoying a much-needed day off.

Muddle the sugar syrup, one mint sprig, and the bourbon in a rocks glass. Add crushed ice and garnish with the remaining mint sprigs.

Glass

Rocks

Garnish

Mint sprigs

Ingredients

½ oz/15ml sugar syrup
(see page 7)

3 fresh mint sprigs

2¼oz/60ml bourbon

the roys

The HBO drama *Succession* is all about the flex. For the Roy family, who all seem to enjoy cocktail hour, the only fitting drink is one that clearly features one star, and here it's Scotch whisky (although any whiskey will do, technically). Although the cocktail has a supporting cast of staples (sweet vermouth, bitters, and a bit of lemon), a good Scotch is really the only way to bring them all in line to produce a truly exceptional drink.

Add all the ingredients to a mixing glass filled with ice and stir gently with a barspoon. Strain into a chilled rocks glass filled with ice and garnish with a thin piece of lemon zest.

Glass

Rocks

Garnish

Lemon zest

Ingredients

2oz/50ml Scotch whisky

⅔ oz/20ml sweet vermouth

a dash of Angostura bitters

striking vipers

Glass

Coupe

Garnish

Apple slice with a drop of bitters on it

Ingredients

1 egg white

1½oz/40ml Calvados

½ oz/15ml yuzu juice

20ml/²⁄₃ oz sugar syrup (see page 7)

1 barspoon absinthe

1 barspoon matcha green-tea powder

a dash of apple juice

At one time, this show's dystopian storylines felt more like a distant world, and less like reality. But then 2020 came along…. One of *Black Mirror*'s most memorable episodes is "Striking Vipers," based around two friends and the anonymity of virtual reality. If you go on a *Black Mirror* binge-fest with your bestie, whip up a few of these… with caution.

Put the egg white in a shaker and stir to break it down (the egg white gives a lovely, rounded, silky texture to the cocktail). Add the rest of the ingredients and ice. Shake, then strain into a glass. Garnish with the slice of apple.

hawaiian punch

In the history of television, many shows have taken the opportunity to work a family trip to Hawaii into their storyline. This includes: *The Brady Bunch*, *Full House*, *Growing Pains*, *Saved by the Bell*, *Beverly Hills 90210*, and even *The Beverly Hillbillies*. *Modern Family* was the first sitcom to do it in quite some time. This Hawaiian Punch is a mix of sherbet, pineapple juice, and soda water or lemon soda. One recipe will and should make enough for the Dunphy-Pritchard-Tucker-Delgado crew.

Cover a muffin tin with plastic wrap. Scoop the sherbet/sorbet into round scoops and put into muffin tins to freeze solid for the punch. When ready to make the punch, pour the pineapple juice and vodka into a punch bowl. Combine and then add the Fruit Punch and ginger ale, adjusting to taste. When ready to serve, remove the sherbet balls from the freezer and place in the punch bowl. Serve immediately.

Glass

Punch cup

Ingredients

Makes: 4-6 glasses

½–1 bottle vodka or rum

1 x 48-oz/1.4-liter container of pineapple, lime, or coconut sherbet/sorbet

1 large can of pineapple juice

6 cups/1.5 liters Fruit Punch

4 cups/1 liter ginger ale

the french tuck

This made-over version of *Queer Eye for the Straight Guy* features five fellas who help make over extraordinary people with compelling stories to tell. The new show focuses on more than just the outward appearance and includes home makeovers, help with cooking, and a little bit of tough love. The French Tuck is not only a good accompaniment to watching this show (along with a box of Kleenex), it's also a stylish way to tuck in your shirt.

Glass

Martini

Ingredients

2oz/50ml vodka

a large dash of Chambord (or crème de mure)

3oz/75ml pineapple juice

Add all the ingredients to a shaker filled with ice, shake sharply, and then strain into a frosted martini glass.

blood and sand

The beautiful beaches and winding roads of Route One in Monterey, California provide the backdrop for this high-production-values HBO show based on the novel of the same name by Laine Moriarty. With many deep, dark, and twisted storylines, a drink with a name like Blood and Sand is the only way to sum up this show's mixture of suspense and beautiful coastal backdrops.

Add all the ingredients to a shaker filled with ice, shake sharply, then strain into a frosted martini glass.

Glass
Martini

Ingredients
1oz/25ml Scotch whisky

1oz/25ml sweet vermouth

1oz/25ml cherry brandy

1oz/25ml orange juice

the liz lemon drop

Glass

Shot

Garnish

Lemon slice

Ingredients

2oz/50ml lemon vodka

½ oz/15ml Cointreau

⅔ oz/20ml fresh
lemon juice

Like Tina Fey's character on *30 Rock*, the Liz Lemon Drop is a real straightshooter. The drink can be presented as a shot or a cocktail. If you want to go all Spring Break with it, you can dip the lemon slice in the Cointreau and set it aflame when you garnish. Either way, this drink is for all the Lizbian's out there. Rejoice!

Add all the ingredients to a shaker filled with ice. Shake very hard and strain into a shot glass. Garnish with a lemon slice.

li'l yoda

Disney+ got a lot of props this year when it released a bevy of programming ahead of schedule during the early days of the pandemic: *Frozen 2* **and** *Onward* **were two standouts. However, the real hit from Disney+ was a TV show based on** *Star Wars*. *The Mandalorian* **is what's known as a Space Western and is the first live-action version of any** *Star Wars* **storyline. One of the best parts of the show is the infant commonly known as little, baby, Yoda. This drink pays homage to the Lucas franchise's most beloved character.**

Shake all the ingredients over ice, strain into a frosted martini glass and serve.

Glass

Martini

Ingredients

1oz/25ml white crème de menthe

½ oz/15ml crème de menthe

1oz/25ml light/ single cream

scandal in belgravia

Scandal in Belgravia pays homage to one of the most well-known stories featuring Sir Arthur Conan Doyle's famed protagonist, Sherlock Holmes, and his assistant, Dr. Watson. Like Holmes, it's a very elusive cocktail with many variations. Take away the grenadine, and you have what's known as a Frostbite. Sub in blue curaçao for grenadine and you have a Baby Blue Silk Stocking.

Glass	Ingredients
Hurricane	1¼oz/35ml gold tequila
	½ oz/15ml white crème de cacao
Garnish	½ oz/15ml grenadine
2 fresh raspberries	½ oz/15ml heavy/ double cream
	a blender

Add all the ingredients to a blender. Add two scoops of crushed ice and blend for 20 seconds. Pour the mixture into a hurricane glass, garnish with two raspberries and serve with two straws (optional).

farm boy swill

Glass

Martini

Full disclosure: this Farm Boy Swill does not contain beet vodka, but it is red and it does contain rum, which is exactly the sort of drink that is really more Dwight Schrute's speed than anything. Additionally, as someone who went to college in the Midwest American Farmland, I assure you that Farm Boy Swill definitely includes Bacardi, a red or purple juice, and maybe a misplaced cigarette butt. Hopefully not.

Ingredients

2oz/50ml Bacardi white rum

3 barspoons grenadine

⅔ oz/20ml fresh lime juice

Shake all the ingredients sharply over ice, then strain into a chilled martini glass and serve.

THE X-FILES

the phyllis h. paddock

Glass

Shot

Ingredients

1 white sugar cube

½ lime

2oz/50ml vodka

a dash of Grand Marnier

1oz/25ml Chambord

Most teachers are underpaid. This episode of *The X-Files* gives a deep insight into the life of a substitute teacher, but this one is actually a demon incarnate, who rips a student's eyes and heart out, forces another to take their life, and if it that wasn't bad enough, takes control of a snake! Her heart is a haze of darkness, which is what you should drink if you are going to binge *The X-Files*.

Put a sugar cube and the fresh lime half, cut into quarters, into a shaker and crush them together with a muddler or barspoon. Add the vodka and Grand Marnier. Fill the shaker with ice, then shake and strain the mixture into a chilled shot glass. Float a single measure of Chambord on to the drink and serve.

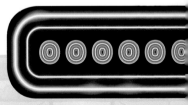

I LOVE LUCY

cuban libre
and ginger rum

I Love Lucy is definitely one of those TV shows that holds up. It's still genuinely laugh-out-loud funny, no matter how many times you watch it. Its stars, Lucille Ball and her Cuban American husband Desi Arnaz, were an unlikely pair, but together had the kind of chemistry that only a Hollywood romance of the golden era can have. The Cuban Libre, is one of the oldest cocktails out there. It allegedly dates back to 1898 when, before the invention of Coca-Cola, it was made by mixing rum and brown sugar. The Ginger Rum is a drink for redhead Lucy— classic, spicy, and unforgettable.

GINGER RUM

Glass

Collins

Garnish

Lime wedge

Ingredients

1 piece stem ginger, crushed to a purée with a fork

1 barspoon ginger syrup from the jar

2¼oz/60ml golden rum

½oz/15ml fresh lime juice

Put the puréed stem ginger, ginger syrup, rum, and lime juice into a shaker filled with ice. Shake well, then strain into a glass filled with ice and garnish with a wedge of lime. Add extra syrup if you prefer a sweeter drink. Alternatively, whizz in a blender, then strain over ice. For a long drink, serve in a Collins glass topped with ginger ale or soda.

CUBAN LIBRE

Glass

Highball

Ingredients

2oz/50ml white rum

1 lime

cola, to top up

Pour the rum into a highball glass filled with ice. Cut a lime into eighths, squeeze and drop the wedges into the glass. Top with cola and serve with straws (optional).

Pictured above.

hot ham water

Glass

Tankard

Garnish

Lemon zest

Cloves

Ingredients

2oz/50ml Scotch whisky

²⁄₃oz/20ml dark honey

1oz/25ml fresh
lemon juice

a pinch of ground
cinnamon or
1 cinnamon stick

boiling water, to top up

Probably… no definitely the most appetizing and posh sounding cocktail in the book—not! That being said, this cocktail does not contain ham, or any animals—it's really a hot toddy. When the weather gets crisp, this is the perfect pairing for a night of binging the Bluths.

Add all the ingredients to a heatproof glass or pewter tankard and stir gently to mix. Top up with boiling water and serve garnished with a piece of lemon zest studded with cloves.

jacoby's coconut

The drink that will help beat any warm-weather blues is Jacoby's Coconut, named after Dr. Jacoby and the little coconut he talks to in his office. Is there any other drink as whimsical as the Piña Colada? An ode to the classic Hawaiian "umbrella" drink, make sure when this is served that you do as Dr. Jacoby does, and date and keep your umbrellas. (And go easy on the golden rum if you want to make it through a proper *Twin Peaks* binge!)

Glass	Ingredients
Sour or Collins	2oz/50ml golden rum
	1oz/25ml coconut cream
Garnish	½ oz/15ml light/single
Slice of pineapple	cream
	1oz/25ml pineapple juice
	a blender

Put all the ingredients into a blender, add a scoop of crushed ice and blend. Pour into a sour or collins glass and garnish with a segment from a thick slice of pineapple.

fish fingers and custard

Fish Fingers and Custard… it still sounds more appetizing than "Hot Ham Water". Although it seems like it could be from *The Office*, this is actually a *Doctor Who* reference. Fish fingers and custard were enjoyed by the Eleventh Doctor not long after his regeneration, when Amy Pond offered him a variety of dishes from her kitchen and the Doctor discovered a particular liking for this odd combination. Note: This drink contains no fish. Or fingers. Just bourbon and caramel.

Blend the ice cream, chocolate milk, sea salt and bourbon in a blender, adding ice depending on how thick you want your shake. Pour into tumblers.

Glass

Tumbler

Ingredients

For 4 people:

4 cups/1 litre salted caramel ice cream

1 cup/250ml chocolate milk

1 teaspoon sea salt

⅔ cup/150ml bourbon

a blender

the festivus
(for the rest of us)

Have you already got a leg-up on Festivus this year? If not, well what are you waiting for? Break out your Festivus pole, get your wrestling gear out, tell Aunt Phyllis what you really think of her, and serve up a batch of this Festivus cocktail. Also known as the Anti-Nog, this not jolly at all drink uses Madeira, Cognac and Jamaican rum to warm you up for a laugh, making you the kind of drunk who's more honest than you should be, and better at wrestling than you may have ever imagined.

Add all the ingredients to a cocktail shaker and shake vigorously for 15 seconds. Pour into a glass, grate over a little nutmeg and serve.

Glass
Tumbler

Garnish
Grated nutmeg

Ingredients
1oz/25ml Madeira wine

½ oz/15ml Cognac

½ oz/15ml Jamaican rum

a pinch of ground cinnamon

1 tablespoon superfine/ caster sugar

1 egg

1oz/25ml heavy/ double cream

Index

Credits

Recipes by: Dog 'n' Bone Books 25, 32; Ursula Ferrigno 20; Laura Gladwin 36; Carol Hilker 10, 11, 12, 18, 49, 62; Elsa Petersen-Schepelern 46, 58; Ben Reed 8, 13, 16, 17, 19, 22, 23, 24, 26, 27, 28, 29, 30, 32, 34, 37, 38, 39, 41, 42, 44, 44, 47, 50, 51, 52, 53, 54, 55, 56, 59, 60, 61, 63; William Yeoward 31, 48
Photography by: Jan Baldwin 21; Peter Cassidy 62; Gavin Kingcome 31, 48, 50; Adrian Lawrence 36; William Lingwood 13, 19, 22, 27, 29, 30, 35, 39, 41, 43, 45, 46, 47, 53, 54, 55, 57, 59, 60, 61, 63; Gareth Morgans 9, 23, 26, 39; Martin Norris 16, 17, 25, 32